"Some women choose to follow men, and some women choose to follow their dreams. If you're wondering which way to go, remember that your career will never wake up and tell you that it doesn't love you anymore."

— Lady Gaga, American musician

"Power is not given to you.
You have to take it."

—Beyoncé Knowles, American musician

"We realize the importance of
our voices only
when we are silenced."

— Malala Yousafzai,
Pakistani activist and Nobel laureate

"If the first woman God ever made was strong enough to turn the world upside down all alone, these together ought to be able to turn it back and get it right side up again."

— Sojourner Truth, American abolitionist

"We realize the importance of "If it's a good idea, go ahead and do it. It's much easier to apologize than it is to get permission."

— Grace Hopper, U.S. Naval Admiral and computer scientist

"I do not wish [women] to have power over men; but over themselves."

— Mary Wollstonecraft, English writer and philosopher

"I do know one thing about me: I don't measure myself by others' expectations or let others define my worth."

— Sonia Sotomayor, associate justice of the U.S. Supreme Court

"The first problem for all of us, men and women, is not to learn, but to unlearn. We are filled with the popular wisdom of several centuries just past, and we are terrified to give it up."

— Gloria Steinem, American activist

"What makes you different or weird, that's your strength."

— Meryl Streep, American actress

"How wonderful it is that nobody need wait a single moment before starting to improve the world."

— Anne Frank, German diarist

"Above all, be the heroine of your life, not the victim."

— Nora Ephron, American writer and filmmaker

"A man who will be intimidated by me is exactly the type of man I have no interest in."

— Chimamanda Ngozi Adichie, Nigerian author

"A woman with a voice is, by definition, a strong woman."

— Melinda Gates, American philanthropist

"I myself have never been able to find out precisely what feminism is: I only know that people call me a feminist whenever I express sentiments that differentiate me from a doormat or a prostitute."

— Chimamanda Ngozi Adichie,
Nigerian author

"I am not free while any woman is unfree, even when her shackles are very different from my own."

— Audre Lorde, American writer and civil rights activist

"Women belong in all places where decisions are being made... It shouldn't be that women are the exception."

— Ruth Bader Ginsburg, associate justice of the U.S. Supreme Court

"I'm not afraid of storms, for I'm learning to sail my ship."

— Louisa May Alcott, author of Little Women

"I will not have my life narrowed down. I will not bow down to somebody else's whim or to someone else's ignorance."

— bell hooks, American author and activist

"Men, their rights, and nothing more; women, their rights, and nothing less."

— Susan B. Anthony, American suffragist

"It took me quite a long time to develop a voice, and now that I have it, I am not going to be silent."

— Madeleine Albright, Former U.S. Secretary of State

"I attribute my success to this: I never gave or took an excuse."

— Florence Nightingale,
the founder of modern nursing

"Don't let anyone rob you of your imagination, your creativity, or your curiosity. It's your place in the world; it's your life."

— Dr. Mae Jemison, engineer, physician, and NASA astronaut

"It is impossible to live without failing at something, unless you live so cautiously that you might as well not have lived at all – in which case, you fail by default."

— J. K. Rowling, British novelist

"You must learn to be still in the midst of activity and to be vibrantly alive in repose."

— Indira Gandhi, first female prime minister of India

The enemy is not lipstick, but guilt itself; we deserve lipstick, if we want it, AND free speech; we deserve to be sexual AND serious – or whatever we please."

— Naomi Wolf, American author and journalist

"Words have power. TV has power. My pen has power."

— Shonda Rhimes, American television producer and screenwriter

"You don't have to be pretty. You don't owe prettiness to anyone."

—Erin McKean, American lexicographer

"Don't compromise yourself.
You are all you've got."

— Janis Joplin, American musician

"I may sometimes be willing to teach for nothing, but if paid at all, I shall never do a man's work for less than a man's pay."

— Clara Barton, founder of the American Red Cross

"I know for sure that what we dwell on is what we become."

— Oprah Winfrey, American media magnate and philanthropist

"I would venture to guess that Anon, who wrote so many poems without signing them, was often a woman."

— Virginia Woolf, English writer

"It's not your job to like me,
it's mine."

— Byron Katie, American speaker and author

"Always be a first-rate version of yourself instead of a second-rate version of somebody else."

— Judy Garland, American singer and actress

"I decided I can't pay a person to rewind time, so I may as well get over it." -

— Serena Williams, an American professional tennis player.

"'Restore connection' is not just
for devices, it is for people too.
If we cannot disconnect,
we cannot lead."

— Arianna Huffington, a Greek-American author,
syndicated columnist, and businesswoman

"I just want women to always feel in control. Because we're capable, we're so capable."

-Nicki Minaj, rapper, singer, songwriter, actress, and model

"My best successes came on the heels of failures."

— Barbara Corcoran,
an American businesswoman, investor, speaker

"We must believe that we are gifted for something, and that this thing, at whatever cost, must be attained."

-Marie Curie, a Polish and naturalized-French physicist and chemist

"Because I am a woman, I must make unusual efforts to succeed. If I fail, no one will say, "She doesn't have what it takes." They will say, "Women don't have what it takes."

— Clare Boothe Luce,
an American author, politician

"You take your life in your own hands, and what happens? A terrible thing, no one to blame."

-Erica Jong, an American novelist, satirist, and poet

"Stop wearing your wishbone where your backbone ought to be."

— Elizabeth Gilbert, an American author

"Courage starts with showing up and letting ourselves be seen."

—Brené Brown, an American research professor

"You may encounter many defeats, but you must not be defeated. In fact, it may be necessary to encounter the defeats, so you can know who you are, what you can rise from, how you can still come out of it."

— Maya Angelou,
an American poet, singer, memoirist,
and civil rights activist

"People think at the end of the day that a man is the only answer [to fulfillment]. Actually a job is better for me."

—Diana, Princess of Wales

"The question isn't who's going to let me; it's who is going to stop me."

— Ayn Rand,
a Russian-American writer and philosopher.

"The way to right wrongs is to turn the light of truth upon them."

-Ida B. Wells, an African-American investigative journalist

"A woman is like a tea bag – you never know how strong she is until she gets in hot water."

— Ayn Rand,
a Russian-American writer and philosopher.

"Life shrinks or expands in proportion to one's courage."

-Anaïs Nin, a French-Cuban American diarist, essayist, novelist, and writer of short stories and erotica.

"Champions keep playing until they get it right."

— Billie Jean King,
an American former World
No. 1 professional tennis player

"Dreams and reality are opposites. Action synthesizes them."

-Assata Shakur, a former member of the Black Liberation Army,

Printed in Great Britain
by Amazon